REGIONAL WILD AMERICA

UNIQUE ANIMALS OF
HAWAII

By Tanya Lee Stone

BLACKBIRCH PRESS

An imprint of Thomson Gale, a part of The Thomson Corporation

THOMSON

GALE

Detroit • New York • San Francisco • San Diego • New Haven, Conn. • Waterville, Maine • London • Munich

For Liza, my Sunshine Girl!

Photo Credits: page 3 © Kennan Ward/CORBIS; pages 5, 14 Corel; page 6 © Stephen Frink/CORBIS; page 7 © Amos Nachoum/CORBIS; page 8 © Mark A. Johnson/CORBIS; page 9 © Stuart Westmorland/CORBIS; page 10 © David Fleetham/Visuals Unlimited; page 11 © John Francis/CORBIS (top), © Jonathan Blair/CORBIS (bottom); page 12 © James Watt/Visuals Unlimited; page13 © Jonathan Blair/CORBIS; pages 15, 16, 17 Thomas Dove; pages 18, 19, 22 Peter LaTourrette/birdphotography.com; pages 20, 21 Honolulu Zoo/honoluluzoo.org; page 23 Ned Friary/Lonely Planet Images

LIBRARY OF CONGRESS CATALOGING-IN-PUBLICATION DATA

Stone, Tanya Lee.
  Unique animals of Hawaii / by Tanya Lee Stone.
    p. cm. — (Regional wild America)
  Includes bibliographical references and index.
  ISBN 1-4103-0087-0 (hard cover : alk. paper)
  1. Animals—Hawaii—Juvenile literature. I. Title II. Series: Stone, Tanya Lee.
Regional wild America.

Contents

Northwestern Hawaiian Islands

PEARL AND HERMES REEF

LAYSAN ISLAND

LISIANSKI ISLAND

MARO REEF

GARDNER PINNACLES

NECKER ISLAND

Pacific Ocean

FRENCH FRIGATE SHOALS

NIHOA

Main Hawaiian Islands

KAUAI

NIIHAU

OAHU

MOLOKAI

★
Honolulu

MAUI

LANAI

KAHOOLAWE

Pacific Ocean

HAWAII

Introduction

The Hawaiian Islands are a group of islands in the Pacific Ocean. There are eight major islands and more than one hundred little ones. The largest island is Hawaii. It is often called the Big Island. The Hawaiian Islands are home to a variety of animals. The first three animals in this book—a fish, a whale, and a sea turtle—all travel by swimming. They are commonly found in the Hawaiian Islands. But they swim to other places as well! The rest of the animals in this book live only in the Hawaiian Islands. Many of them are endangered. This means they are in danger of becoming extinct.

The Hawaiian Islands are home to many endangered animals.

Fish Face!

The name of Hawaii's unofficial state fish is a tongue twister! Its Hawaiian name is Humu-humu-nuku-nuku-apua 'a. This means "fish with a pig-nosed face" or "fish with the snout of a pig." The fish often noses around in a reef, turning over rocks with its snout. And it makes a grunting sound when it is bothered!

The pig-nosed triggerfish uses its snout to explore the shallow reef waters.

This fish has many common names. Two of them are the pig-nosed triggerfish and the painted triggerfish. The fish lives in the waters off the Hawaiian Islands. It also swims south to Australia and west through the East Indies all the way to Africa. This colorful creature has black, yellow, red, blue, and green markings on its body.

The spine on its back helps a triggerfish escape from predators.

The pig-nosed triggerfish grows to about 10 inches (25 cm) in length. It is not a fast swimmer, but it is a good hunter. It can easily dart forward and backward. It swims along the bottom of shallow reef waters looking for food. The pig-nosed triggerfish has strong jaws and sharp teeth. It eats worms, snails, and sea urchins. Other foods include shrimp, clams, small fish, and algae. It also has a good way to protect itself from being hunted. Like other triggerfishes, it has a spine on the top of its body. The fish can get into a hole or other tight spot and use this "trigger" to make itself stuck. Once it does this, an enemy is unable to pull the triggerfish out.

Every humpback whale has a unique pattern on the underside of its fluke.

A Whale of a Tail!

Humpback whales swim in both the Atlantic and Pacific oceans. Thousands of them spend October to April in Hawaii. There, they swim in the calm waters and have their babies. The humpback whale is the official marine mammal of Hawaii.

When humpbacks swim near the surface, they often dive. You can see a humpback's tail (fluke) come up out of the water when it dives. The pattern of black and white on the underside of its tail is unique to each animal. Humpback whales also jump right out of the water! This is called breaching. Humpbacks sometimes swim on their backs with their flippers in the air. Their flippers are much longer than those of other whales.

Even though this huge humpback may weigh 40 tons when it breaches, it is able to leap high out of the water.

Humpbacks are huge. They weigh up to 25 to 40 tons (23 to 36 metric tons) and stretch 50 feet (15 m) long! That's bigger than a school bus! Although the whales are very big, the food they eat is tiny. Humpbacks mainly eat tiny plants and animals called plankton. They also eat other small fish. A humpback is one of four kinds of baleen whales. Instead of teeth, these whales have big, brushy plates in their mouth called baleen. When a humpback opens its mouth, water floods in. The whale uses its tongue to push the water back out through the baleen, and the food stays inside. It is kind of like pouring spaghetti through a strainer.

Males make a kind of singing sound. These songs last about twenty minutes and are often sung over and over for hours. Some scientists think males sing to attract females. Humpbacks may also communicate with each other by slapping the water with their tails or flippers.

Turtles in Trouble

Hawaiian green sea turtles live a very long time—up to eighty years! Their Hawaiian name is Honu. This reptile is the biggest hard-shelled sea turtle in the world. Like those of other sea turtles, their flipperlike limbs are perfect for swimming. A turtle's top shell is called the carapace. Adult Hawaiian green sea turtles can have carapaces more than 3 feet (0.9 m) in length. These turtles also weigh about 400 pounds (182 kg). Males have much longer tails than females.

Hawaiian green sea turtles can live to be more than seventy years old.

Every two to three years, the Hawaiian green sea turtle swims up to 700 miles (1,126 km) from the main islands of Hawaii to the French Frigate Shoals in the Northwestern Hawaiian Islands. They travel there to mate and lay their eggs. When females are ready to lay their eggs, they pull themselves out of the water and onto the

A green sea turtle spends most of her life in the water, but comes to shore to lay her eggs in the sand (below).

beach using their front flippers. Once they choose a nesting spot, they dig a hole with their back flippers. A clutch, or group of eggs, is laid in the hole at night. Females lay five or six clutches during a breeding season. Each clutch has 100 to 120 eggs.

After she lays her eggs, a female covers them with dirt to protect them. After about sixty days, the eggs hatch at night. The hatchlings, or baby turtles, dig their

way out of the egg pit together. Once on the surface, they scramble down the beach to get into the water. Young turtles are omnivorous, which means they eat both meat and plants. Adults mainly eat algae and sea grass. These sea turtles are protected by law. It is illegal to hurt, kill, or catch them.

Mysterious Monk

Hawaiian monk seals are mainly found off the northwestern islands of Hawaii. There are few, if any, people to bother them there. Some people believe this seal got its common name because it keeps to itself, much like monks do. Others believe the name came from the loose skin at the back of the seals' necks that looks like the hood of a monk's robe. The Hawaiian name for this seal is Ilio-holo-i-ka-uaua. It means, "dog that runs in rough waters."

This Hawaiian monk seal pup will be about 7 feet long and weigh about 400 pounds when it is fully grown.

These marine mammals grow to about 7 feet (2 m) long and weigh about 400 pounds (182 kg). They eat fish, octopus, certain kinds of eel, and lobster. They sometimes spend days in the open ocean feeding. Hawaiian Monk seals can dive to depths of 500 feet (152 m) when searching for food. They can stay underwater for up to twenty minutes. Their torpedo-shaped bodies, waterproof coats, and flippers all make them well suited for the sea. On land, it is much harder for them to move their heavy bodies across the sand.

Monk seals do come on land to rest. Females also climb onto the beach to have their babies, or pups. Most females give birth to one pup every two years. Pups nurse for about six weeks. The pups weigh about 30 pounds (14 kg) when they are born. By the time a pup stops nursing, it will weigh up to 200 pounds (91 kg).

Hawaiian monk seals are an endangered species. There are only about 1,200 to 1,500 of them left. The seals are easily disturbed by people. In fact, people watching a mother can cause it to leave its pup's side. It is best to admire these animals from a distance.

It is hard for monk seals to drag their heavy bodies across the sand, but they do come onto the beach to rest and give birth.

Hawaiian short-eared owls make their nests on the ground, so they need to have sharp eyesight and a keen sense of sound to avoid predators like cats and mongooses.

Pueo the Protector

The pueo, or Hawaiian short-eared owl, is found all over the main Hawaiian Islands. It has also been seen on the northwestern islands. It lives near the coast as well as in the mountains. This owl often flies much higher than most owls. And unlike many owls, the pueo makes its nest on the ground. Baby owls are often killed by cats and mongooses that get to the nest. People also disturb this owl's habitat.

The Hawaiian short-eared owl is between 13 and 17 inches (33 to 43 cm) tall. Females are slightly bigger than males. The owl has a round face and large yellow eyes. Its body feathers are brown and whitish. Most owls are nocturnal (active at night). But the pueo is active at dawn, dusk, and during the middle of the day. Like other owls, the pueo is an excellent hunter. It has sharp eyesight and a keen sense of hearing. Owls also have strong, soft wing feathers. This makes their flight very quiet and lets them sneak up on small animals. Feathers on their legs also help silence their flying. The pueo eats small rodents such as mice and rats. It will also eat some insects and small birds.

Hawaiian legend tells of this owl keeping people from harm. It is called the Protector. Today, though, it is the pueo that needs to be protected. It is in danger of becoming extinct. The number of pueo on the island of Oahu has gotten so low that this owl is now an endangered animal.

Fit for a Flower

The 'I'iwi is one kind of Hawaiian songbird. It has many kinds of calls. Many of the sounds it makes are quite loud. Some calls are alarms. Others are to attract a mate, or are a signal to look for food. Both males and females sing.

This forest bird is a common sight on the islands of Hawaii, Maui, and Kauai. It likes to fly in the higher parts of the forest. It is rarely seen near the ground. This bird's bill makes it easy to identify. The bill is long, curved, and red or peach colored. The bird uses its bill to drink nectar from flowers. It hops from branch to branch. It can drink the nectar from many flowers in just a few minutes. The 'I'iwi also eats larvae, insects, and spiders.

Bright red 'I'iwis like the upper canopy of the Hawaiian forests.

This small bird is about 5 or 6 inches (13 to 15 cm) long. Males are a bit larger than females. The 'I'iwi has pink legs and a black tail. Its wings are also black with some patches of white. The 'I'iwi's body feathers are bright red. Long ago, its beautiful feathers were used to make capes for Hawaiian royalty.

A male and female pair of these songbirds stays together during breeding season. They build a nest, and both parents care for the young. Parents defend their chicks from predators such as rats, cats, hawks, and owls. Chicks grow yellowish green feathers. Their bright red feathers develop by the time they are adults.

An 'I'iwi uses its long, curved bill to drink nectar from flowers.

The nene is an endangered bird.

Nimble Nene

Hawaii's state bird is the Hawaiian goose. Its Hawaiian name is nene. The nene is related to the Canada goose. These geese once lived on all the main Hawaiian Islands. Today, they are mainly found on the Big Island. The nene is a large bird. It averages about 2 feet (0.6 m) in length. A nene has a black head and beak. Its cheeks and neck have ivory feathers.

The Hawaiian goose is different from other geese. A nene's wings are not very strong. This may be because they do not fly as much as other geese. They also do not spend much time swimming. A nene has longer toes than other geese. Its feet are not as webbed. This helps the bird walk easily over the rough, rocky lava flows where it lives.

Nenes eat grasses, leaves, flowers, fruits, seeds, and other plant materials. They feed while walking through grassy and shrubby areas. When a female nene is ready to lay her eggs, she builds a nest. She lines it with her soft downy feathers. She lays two to five eggs. The young geese cannot fly for about twelve weeks.

In the past, people have hunted these birds for both food and sport. They have also taken over nene habitat by building on it. Nenes have been hurt by animals that are not native to Hawaii. Dogs, cats, pigs, rats, and mongooses were brought to Hawaii over time. These animals hunt and kill nenes, as well as other animals. There are only about 500 to 800 of these birds left today. They are on the endangered species list.

Nenes eat flowers, leaves, and plants while they walk through grassy areas.

Acro-BAT-ics!

Since the only way to get to Hawaii is to swim or fly, most mammals that live there were brought by people. Only one land mammal is native to Hawaii. It is the Hawaiian hoary bat. Its Hawaiian name is 'Ope 'ape 'a. Bats are the only kind of mammal that can fly. Bat wings do not have feathers like bird wings. Their wings are made of a thin skin. The skin begins at the ankles and stretches out over a bat's long fingers. Hawaiian hoary bats have wings that spread almost 12 inches (30 cm) across when open. They fold their wings up like an umbrella when they sleep.

The Hawaiian hoary bat is the only land mammal that is native to Hawaii.

Hawaiian hoary bats have thick brown and white fur. They are related to North American hoary bats. North American hoary bats migrate, or travel, to warmer areas when the weather turns cold. But Hawaiian hoary bats do not migrate. This may be because the mild Hawaiian weather suits them year-round. These bats live on several of the Hawaiian Islands. They are mostly seen on Hawaii and Kauai, though.

The body of a hoary bat can fit in a person's hand, but its wings are about a foot wide when open.

Bats are nocturnal. Like many kinds of bats, hoary bats roost (sleep) upside down. They often go back to the same trees to roost each day before the sun comes up. Hawaiian hoary bats keep to themselves. When evening comes, a bat flies off on its own to hunt. They mainly eat night-flying insects. These bats can be seen diving, twisting, and turning as they catch moths, beetles, and other insects midflight!

Bats are not blind. But it is not their eyes that make them such great night fliers! Like other bats, Hawaiian hoary bats make high-pitched sounds that humans cannot usually hear. These sounds hit objects and then bounce back to a bat's ears—like an echo. The echoes tell the bat where an object is. They also tell the bat how big something is and how fast it is traveling. This amazing talent is called echolocation. It makes bats very efficient hunters!

Standing on Stilts

The Hawaiian stilt bird is a rare and beautiful sight. Its Hawaiian name is Ae 'o. As it flies, its long pinkish legs trail behind it. When it lands, it makes sure every nearby water bird knows to get out of its way. The Hawaiian stilt bird announces its landing with a loud pip-pip-pip!

This bird has a small body, but it stands 16 inches (41 cm) tall. The top of its head and neck are black. Black feathers also cover its back. Females have a bit of brown on their backs, too. The underside of the Hawaiian stilt bird is a snowy white.

A Hawaiian stilt bird wades through wetlands on its long, thin, pinkish legs.

The Ae 'o uses its stiltlike legs to wade through ponds, wetlands, and mudflats. As it wades, it eats. The Hawaiian stilt bird has a long, thin, black beak. It uses its long beak to pluck food from shallow water. These birds eat fish, crabs, worms, shrimp, and other small sea life. They also snatch up water insects.

Animals that hunt the Hawaiian stilt bird include rats, cats, dogs, and mongooses. Loss of habitat has also taken its toll. The Hawaiian stilt bird is endangered. There are only about 1,200 to 1,600 of them in the wild.

Its long, thin beak makes it easy for the stilt bird to catch fish, shrimp, worms, and insects in the shallow water of ponds and mudflats.

Many unique animals live in and around the Hawaiian Islands. They all add to the richness and beauty of this tropical paradise. Conservation efforts are underway to help many of the endangered animals of Hawaii. There is hope that in time, their numbers will grow strong again.

Glossary

Baleen Large, brushlike structures in a baleen whale's mouth.
Breaching When a whale jumps out of the water.
Carapace The top of a turtle's shell.
Clutch Group of eggs.
Echolocation Locating objects using echoes.

Fluke A whale's tail.
Hatchling A baby turtle.
Mollusk A soft-bodied animal without a skeleton.
Nocturnal Active at night and asleep during the day.
Predator An animal that hunts another animal for food.

For More Information

Goldberg, Jake. *Hawaii.* New York: Marshall Cavendish, 1998.

Haffner, Marianne. *Bats!: Amazing and Mysterious Creatures of the Night.* San Diego, CA: Blackbirch Press, 1998.

Stone, Tanya Lee. *Living World of Blue.* San Diego, CA: Blackbirch Press, 2001.

Sullivan, Jody. *Hawaii.* Mankata, MN: Bridgestone Books, 2003.

Index